So You *Still* Want To Be a Ghost Hunter

By Jason Hess

Published by DragonEye Publishing

So You Still Want To Be A Ghost Hunter
Copyright © 2018 by Jason Hess

All rights reserved. No part of this book may be reproduced, by any means or in any form whatsoever without written permission from the author and Publisher, except for brief quotation embodied in literary articles or reviews.

Publisher info. Contact
DragonEye Publishing
753A Linden Pl.
Elmira, New York, 14901

For Questions Phone: 1-(607)-333-5256

For information about our books, and for special discounts for single / bulk purchases, please contact DragonEye Publishing Ordering Dept. at:
Website: DragonEyePublishers.com
Email: Orders@DragonEyePublishers.com

To request one of our authors for speaking engagements or book signings, please contact DragonEye Publishing Publicity Dept. at: Directors@DragonEyePublishers.com

Published by, an Imprint of DragonEye Publishing

ISBN 13: 978-1-61500-220-7 (Paperback)
ISBN 13: 978-1-61500-221-4 (EBook)

Library of Congress Control Number: 2018955407

DragonEye Publishing First Edition: 2018
First Printing: September 1, 2018

10 9 8 7 6 5 4 3 2 1

Manufactured in the United States of America

Dedicated to all paranormal investigators, Inventors, and researchers

So You Still Want To Be a Ghost Hunter

Table of Contents

5	Preface
7	The Beginning
12	EQUIPMENT
25	Investigating
30	Analyzing
36	The Reveal
38	The Next Case
40	Types of Haunts
43	Conclusion
45	Case Files
49	Glossary of Terms Used

So You Still Want To Be a Ghost Hunter

Preface

I started my research of the paranormal in 2006. I did this to satisfy my own curiosity. I have had personal experiences in the past and had many questions. My mission was to help people thinking they are haunted. My first group has been together also since 2006 and I was a co-founder. I left in 2017. In January 2018 I started a new group. We are a small group we service Illinois and Iowa. But we network with other groups across the country.

With the incredible number of people now interested in the paranormal and the misconception of what we do, we decided to give a few beginning ideas on ghost hunting.

This is a brief book and gives you an idea on the mindset and some equipment that will be needed. A lot of time has been put into our group and money as well. We have made mistakes but overcame them with honors.

Ghost hunting is not for everyone and sometimes an inexperience person can create more problems than solve.

With a general knowledge you can learn and grow as an investigator. But until then it's hard to know what is wrong and what is right.

Please enjoy...

The Beginning

So you still want to be a ghost hunter? This book has similar content to So You Want To Be A Ghost Hunter, but that book is no longer in print. But here is the biggest question. Why? Did you see a television show that got you thinking "Hey I can do that."? Or maybe you want the hell scared out of you? My reasons are things that happened to me in the past and I wanted answers. In fact most of my team researches for the same reason.

If you think what you see on TV is cool, great! But probably two days of investigating and many hours analyzing went into that thirty minute show. A six hours investigation usually takes around sixty hours to go over all the data and maybe we will find around ten minutes that we can present to a client. That is if we find anything at all.

Sometimes what we find is natural to the area. There are other times that we have nothing at all. At that point we keep in contact with the client and see if the activity comes back. If it does we conduct another investigation.

Now you want to be scared? Well in October there are many haunted houses popping up and many theme parks have things that would scare you. And if you really want to be scared I could send you a picture of my ex-wife. Ghost hunting is not the thing to do if you want to be scared. In fact many times you don't know anything changed until you start analyzing the data.

Now that you have a reason, you have to think about how. This is not something you just jump into. Too many people are just running around trying to capture a ghost on film illegally and get in big trouble. Cemeteries may be a great place to start but many states have laws where you cannot be in there after dark. Abandoned buildings always seem creepy, but once again trespassing laws can get you a new pair of bracelets.

The best way that you can start is find a local group and put in an application to join. This way you can learn from their combined knowledge and experience. Plus they should already have equipment for the group to use.

Be careful about choosing a group because there are many fakes just like everywhere else. If the group charges for an investigation, they must know something we don't know. How can you charge for a service that works on theories? If their business card is on a dirty napkin, they are probably going to disband next week after they get money from you.

Now if you want to start your own group, good luck! It's hard and expensive. There is equipment needed, team members, and the most important is a location. The last is the hardest.

A lot of people think if you make a website saying you're a paranormal investigator others will be running towards you. Most of the time they run away from you. Building a reputation is a hard thing to do. There are many skeptics in the world waiting to disprove everything you do. With that you must make sure it's credible and have the evidence unaltered to present to the public.

Since there have been so many shows come and go, this field has really come under attack. So you have to have thick skin and don't let one person ruin it for you. It is way better to agree to disagree then get into a shouting match.

The way we started was doing outside investigations at public locations and also at member's homes as practice investigations. Then the funniest thing happened! Someone wanted us to investigate their house. Then another, and another. We got businesses and even the US Army. How freaking cool is that! We have worked with local government agencies as well. My old group was featured in an online pay per view and on a full length documentary. I have come a long way in the last twelve years.

Many members have been in the groups since the beginning but some have come and gone. Some even started other groups, and others left due to family situations. But we have always been a group that supports each other.

This book was made to help you to get started and to also share some experiences of our group. Ghost hunting isn't for everyone and may not be for you. This will walk you step by step through the beginning stages. We will go through equipment, standard terms, and some basic guidelines. Good luck and happy hunting!

EQUIPMENT

Everyone thinks that there is special equipment that is needed to investigate. Well there is some, but most are items that can be found at a local electronic store. There are some pieces that are harder to get but you can find online. Some can be ten or twenty dollars and others up to three thousand dollars, which we don't have yet.

Now look around the room you're in. If you are like most Americans you may see a computer and a TV. OK, you have already started. Do you have a camera? How about a video camera? You do! Wow! You have the beginning of a paranormal investigators kit.

OK now that you know the common things that some people have we will start talking about some things that are not so easy to find lying around the house.

The first thing we bought as a new group was a voice recorder. This is to capture audio that is not audible to the naked ear. EVP's (electronic voice phenomenon) are voices or sounds that are captured on electronic devices and are usually found after you are done recording. This is also one of the most common pieces of evidence found during an investigation.

Voice recorders that are PC compatible are the best in our mind, for the reason that you can download to your computer and start analyzing within minutes.

For that you need a good sound editing program. These could even be found for free online. We use a program that normally sells in the upward range of three hundred dollars.

Fact some voices or sounds that you can hear can possibly be picked up on your device. But if you do hear a disembodied voice that same recorder may not record it. I know it's weird but true.

So now you have another piece of equipment that will get you started. And as you grow so will your arsenal. But it's always good to have two pieces of data to back up each other.

EMF (electromagnetic field) meters are the next step in your journey. This device detects as it says electromagnetic fields. The theory is that a spirit may create energy when trying to manifest. Other theories are that they pull energy to do the same. Which is correct, well we don't know yet but that disturbance may lead you to some evidence.

Now some meters can read both emf and temperature. This is a great thing to have since heat is energy and if you come up on a cold spot you can read the ambient temperature which we will be talking about in a minute.

There are different types of emfs, ac and dc. Ac is man-made and dc is natural. In cases where there is high power lines or shielded wires in the home a tri-field meter would be a better tool to use.

Remember two pieces of evidence. Say you have a temperature drop and high emf, take a picture with both meters together. And if you just have one meter say it out loud and take a picture. Why say it out loud? Your voice recorder might pick up an evp at the same time. You got your two.

I am going to tell you that we caught while doing that online pay per view. I had a real weird feeling and I ask is someone there. We captured on the voice recorder in my hand a little girl saying help me.

Well I called the person that was doing the pay per view and told her I found something. And she said the same thing. We emailed each other what we found. I was the same voice and the same words. But hers was caught on digital video camera that was being used for a dvr setting for the pay per view.

A few days later I get a call saying another investigator picked up the same thing on his camcorders. Capturing an evp on two devices is hard, but three, I never heard of that happening.

One thing that we have found out is usually something happens in a room we are not in and it's a personal experience or just a story. So the next piece cost a little more but well worth the money.

A standard Closed Circuit Digital Video Recorder system is one of our most valuable pieces of equipment. Most everyone has seen cameras for this and it is used mostly for security reasons. But this way you can have at least four cameras running and you don't have to be near them. Most have an infrared lighting system so you can see in the dark. Also they have a good hard drive in it so it can be left unattended and can be analyzed at a later time. Now remember that you count how long you run your cameras and multiply it by cameras that are being used is the least amount of time to analyze the data.

Now remember that a dvr system is for indoor use only. If you use it outside it could rain, or just the humidity can ruin the hard drive. Just because the Cameras are weather resistant doesn't mean the dvr is....duh.

For outdoors get a handheld Video camera. Also many digital cameras also can film video, but some hand held video cameras have inferred red (ir) illuminators. This commonly is called night vision or low light mode.

With most things, there is a chance to get a false positive. So watch out for ir lighting to cross or to cast a shadow.

Thermometers are the next tool used. Theory behind that is that since a spirit needs energy to manifest, it pulls the heat from the air creating a cold spot. See I told you we would talk about it.

Once again, more on that later. You should have two different types. One is for the ambient air and the other is a non-contact thermometer. Sometimes a cold spot can appear on a surface or free floating. So these thermometers will cover it all.

Thermal cameras are expensive but can see temperature changes on surfaces. You probably seem these on TV but many groups cannot afford most of them. But now they are more affordable and they have some that will connect to your smart phone. Please don't download an app that is used for entertainment purposes.

These cameras are used by home inspectors, fire fighters, the army, and may more. This shows the temperature difference in whatever you look at. For example If the temperature is sixty eight degrees and its sunset you may see some areas holding heat as the air gets cooler. A rock will hold that temperature for a longtime. And what if your buddy walks in front of the camera, you will see a huge difference.

For obvious reasons cold is represented in blues and red is for hot. And there are many colors in between. Ok now say your inside and the wall is showing yet again sixty eight degrees and you see a blue spot right in the middle of the wall. Before jumping to conclusions makes sure there are not any vents or windows near. But that is a huge temperature difference.

Another thing you need to watch is reflective surfaces. It can be your reflection. Or it could pick up a heat signature where someone touched an item.

Sensitives and mediums. Jason why are they with equipment? Well if you were to hold on I would explain. There are two types of sensitive, and one we shall call a fake. These are people that try to call upon your family members that have passed on.

The others, I can't explain. They have a gift that cannot be scientifically recorded. But they may bring you to an area that does have activity. And there capture your evidence. I have only met a few people that may have that gift. And a lot more that are not even close.

Like this one time at band c.... I mean at an outdoor fest A strong storm rolled through overnight. Most tents were standing, but the funny thing is the psychic's tent was blown away. You would have thought that they would have seen that coming.

Also look out for ghost meters or radar...they are for entertainment. But you can download a few apps that are ghost boxes. These scan radio frequencies at a high rate so u can't understand a word. So when a word or a sentence comes through you hope you voice recorder is right there.

There are em pumps that will put some electricity in the air. We have use something similar.

Full spectrum cameras, both video and snap, cameras have the filters, the manufactures put in so you can get a clean picture. Well full spectrum cameras have that filter taken out.

Geophone measures vibrations. This is highly sensitive and may not be a great thing to have or may be an awesome thing. Personally I have yet to try it.

Everyday someone has an idea how to capture proof and develop new gear. But you can capture so much with just the basics

Now that you have the tools needed, you need to learn how to use them. Basically it's all self-explanatory and you don't need me for that. It's a camera, point and shoots. The biggest thing I forget is to hit record, well no one is perfect.

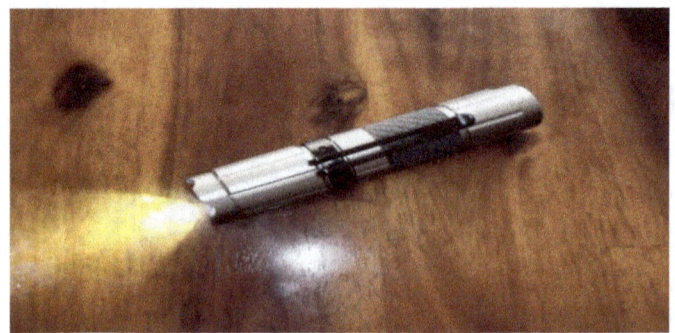

I don't think I need to talk about flash lights but I will. Its dark you need to see. Bring a flash light. Also a laser pointer with a grid tip would be good so if the grid is broken you could see it.

Also make sure you have a way to get to and from. It may look weird you getting on the bus with a few cases of equipment.

Get a storage case. This protects your gear and so you can cart everything around and let's get out there.

Investigating

You got the reason and you got the tool. Then you get an email that someone thinks something strange is going on in their house. What do you do? Think about it I'll wait.........

You got it? Great! I was going to make a sandwich waiting but I will put that on hold.

Well the steps taken are a little more difficult than most think. This is to protect you from wasting time and energy so you can help people that need it. Do you know the facts? What is going on and are the people credible? So you better interview all involved before you go in.

We has a standard interview sheet that our case manager usually goes over with our client before we even set up a date. With this we can see if they are looking for attention, see if they need other help, or may be under the influence. We will almost always set up an investigation to find out what they are experiencing. We have not turned down a case and so far haven't found anyone who wanted to trick us. Nor have we turned down a case due to any other reason.

We also have a permission to investigate form that you need the client to sign. Remember this, because this saves you from trespassing charges.

With the interview done and a date to go to their house in hand, get ready to investigate. Pack up your equipment and make sure you have extra batteries. Try to get premium batteries for a longer battery life. The cheap batteries usually die in a short time. And remember the theory of a spirit pulling energy, well it could drain your batteries as well as pull energy from other electronic devices or yourself.

Make sure you carry yourself in a professional manner at all times. Be respectful during your investigation to the owner and to any possible spirits there. You do not want to anger something that is already scaring the client.

Before you get to the clients make sure that your team signs a personal injury waiver. This protects the client in case someone get hurt.

When you get to the clients house make sure you do a walk through and see if there are high emfs that could cause a natural problem. Electromagnetic hyper sensitivity can cause many different things to different people. This may include hallucinations, skin irritation, headaches, and other things. These can be from natural sources or electrical wiring. This may cause some of the claims from the client. As an investigator you're not trying to prove a haunting but to find an explanation.

During your sweep you can also see where you will set up your equipment and take temperature readings. This will save you time and extra steps during the night. So take your time and don't get confused. Write everything down.

Now let's turn off the lights. Why do you turn off the lights you ask? For the same reason you don't go to a drive in during the day. Since they have to pull energy to appear to us, it is easier to see the apparition in the dark. Now does that mean you can only hunt ghost at night? No it just makes it easier to make a visual capture.

Different groups and investigators conduct investigations differently. But keep your senses open and try to record everything. Ask questions and pause so they can answer. Stay in an area longer than just a few minutes. If you keep moving around you will make it harder to review and you have to be patient. They won't jump out and say "Here I am….take my picture!"

This is why a dvr system with those multiple cameras work great. And if you can place a voice recorder near the camera. Now you have to pieces of equipment in hopes to catch something.

After you think you collected enough data, and maybe had an experience or two, pack up and start analyzing. This is the most difficult part of this field.

Analyzing

Well congrats! Your first investigation is in the books now! It's time to see if you captured anything. Download everything you can to your computer. That way you can burn a disk, transfer to a flash drive or an external hard drive and keep it safe until you're fully done with analyzing everything. We have lost evidence when a computer blows up or the hard drive goes down. This is when people question what you found and how, of course.

Most of the time we will hook up our camcorders and DVR system, to our TV so we have a big screen to watch the video on. Personally I cannot do video work because my attention span isn't too long. Dang! I fall asleep during most movies!

Now with digital cameras no more damaged tapes. Or dvd's to break. Just use and sd card and you can download it to your computer for safe keeping. But remember to back it up.

With your audio, it's best to use audio editing software so you can amplify or slow down your audio. You can download a free editor online and use that until you can save money for a premium program. You can use normal ear buds or do what I did and get DJ headphones.

Now if you hear something out of the ordinary, mark it. Copy it so you can listen to it and use different editing tools to clean it up so even someone that doesn't know what you do can hear it. It's not always so easy, and a clip can be interpreted different ways by different people. So be sure of yourself.

But make sure that you keep the original for people to hear. Then see if they hear the same thing. And let them try and clean it up too.

Usually evps are the most common type of evidence found. But you cannot base a haunting on just audio. You can capture audio anywhere. I really hate to say that since I love doing the audio work. So let's move on to a different medium.

Most camera and computer systems have a picture viewing program. Up load all the pictures you took onto your computer and look through them. With most programs you can at least enlarge the picture so any little disturbance you can see if it's natural or paranormal. Since visual evidence is the hardest to find, when you do capture something jump up and down because most of the time the picture can be debunked.

If you receive a picture from anyone be skeptical about it. When you enlarge the picture you can also see if the pixilation is different. If it is , well it was photo shopped in.

Orbs are the most discussed and thrown out piece of data. Most times it is dust, bugs or moisture. So remember your surroundings and make sure you note the conditions. Even the cleanest of homes could have dust flying around. Often if I don't see dust orbs I find that more paranormal then the rest of the investigation.

If you are at an outdoor location and it starts raining, the orb looks to be flying up and has a tail. It's just rain people.

Mist is another thing captured that might appears in some pictures. You need to ask yourself if someone was smoking, was it cold, or is it my breath. Was the client making popcorn and it burnt? Things like this may cause a mist in the picture that could cause you to scratch your head.

Shadows, faces or full body apparitions are the hardest things to capture. Also these are the easiest things to make a mistake on. See the human brain is a great thing. It can make things look different then what they really are. This is call matrixing, and Keanu isn't going to be there! The brain tries to recognize things it is familiar with, like seeing Jesus on a piece of toast.

Also ask if someone off frame could have cast a shadow from another light source. The hardest to figure out is when there is a full human form right smack dab in the middle of the picture with no explanation. If you got this, consider yourself one of the lucky few in the world to have this.

Now let's move on to video. So get the popcorn and a drink! Sit down and keep the remote in one hand and a pen and note pad in the other. Well maybe forget the popcorn because you will be busy. Our cameras have night vision which uses infrared lights so we cannot see what we are filming unless you look at the little two inch screen.

Once again with shadows be careful because if you have an infrared source behind you and you're filming with night vision you may capture your own shadow and not know it. So be aware of your surroundings. Watch carefully and don't lose the attention that you're giving this data. Once again this is why I don't do it, well I don't much.

Now you're hours in and you found things you cannot explain. Share with other team members and see if they are seeing or hearing the same things as you. They also may have an alternate explanation for the anomaly that you capture.

When you feel confident in your findings, present them to your client. Do not try to scare them but make them feel secure in their home. Explain everything to them and possible reasons behind what you find. You must be honest with your client. Many people just want to know if someone else can feel, hear or see the same things as them and that alone can give them peace of mind.

The Reveal

Now you have your evidence in hand and you're a confident you found things. Well you need to tell your client. If you don't share with them, why did you even start.

This is a hard thing to do especially if you didn't find anything. With that you need to try and explain a logical reason why the client is experiencing these things.

Good luck with that, but they might ask you to come back. At this point try to schedule something up. Please don't leave them hanging. These people asked you for help so try your best to give that to them.

Now if you found something this is great, if it backs up there claims even better. This doesn't have to be paranormal and can be natural. It is still evidence and the client deserves to know this.

If you believe you have found something paranormal then present that to them. But also find out if they feel endangered. If they say they do then direct them to someone who can get rid of this entity.

And now when you are done with all that make sure that the client understands what you found and explain if you need to.

If you did a good job, the word will get out and possibly more people will call on you. This is how you build your reputation.

Oh yeah before you leave the clients place see if you can tell anyone about this. We have a publicity form they sign stating that they want or don't want it to be published. Never use their names or addresses. But if you can put it up on your website or social media page others will see. This can be good or bad. Good because you're getting yourself out there. People will try to discredit what you have found. Listen to them and if you disagree with them stand your ground. But be professional.

The Next Case

Well done your first case is done and you can relax! But do you think you did well? Do you think what you presented is accurate and you're confident that the skeptic will try to tear it apart and it will hold up? If you don't, take a break and review again. It never hurts to keep going over the data.

After all these years we still go over old data and try to learn or see if there was something that we missed. We are human and we make mistakes. Since this field is not a definite science and we work with theories we keep on trying to find a conclusion to this mystery.

Keep learning and sharing with other investigators. Someday we may have proof to prove life after death. Now this is just a brief idea on what to do. As you mature into a seasoned vet you will have your own way on doing things. And maybe someday you will be sitting at your laptop typing out a way you do things.

Now did I share everything? No! Why you may ask? Well I am known as the target in the group. The reason is I provoke and stir up a mess. I do not do this in someone's house but outside.....yeah I can get nasty. As a new investigator I do not condone this.

You need to stay professional and stay strong in your findings. If you have enough evidence to have secured your findings, then skeptics can't beat on you. They will try as will other groups, but stand tall.

Also if you need help as another group, Unity is key in this business. Badmouthing can ruin not just the group that is getting badmouthed but also the group doing all the talking.

Types of Haunts

There are different types of haunting. You didn't know that did you, well there are. Intelligent, residual, poltergeist, and demonic are all different in their own ways.

First we will go over intelligent haunts. These are spirits that can communicate and interact with people. Most often this can be associated with family members or trap spirits trying to find the light. That sounds good but is probably wrong. They can interact and this type of haunt is one that as a ghost hunter you want to investigate because the evidence will mount up.

Residual haunts are easy to define. This is energy that keeps playing over and over. Sometimes you can set your watch to it. It will repeat either hourly, daily, monthly or yearly and so on. This is not trapped souls trying to get to heaven but like a DVD that plays over and over.

Poltergeist, Latin for noisy ghost, is very fascinating and sometime easy to recreate. When someone calls talking about this type of activity, be careful because they are rare to find or to capture. Also if you go to talk to the client and a little blonde girl is sitting in front of the TV, hold in the laughter.

Demonic haunts are not really something you really want to deal with but sometimes necessary. The real things you need to know is how to recognize it. This is something that you will learn and remember for your life if you encounter it. Don't think you as a ghost hunter can get rid of this type of haunt; call a real demonologist and maybe a church.

You may experience warm spots and phantom smells similar to sulfur. There are chances that a haunting of a small child could be demonic since children should pass and leave this plain. Be so very careful on these cases.

So now that you know what kinds of haunting there are, you can tell your client what is happening in their house. So many times people can live with a haunting and will get use to them. If you are unsure call someone that may know to help you. Don't scare the client.

Knowledge is the best tool you have. Learn and do outdoor investigations before you go into a private residence. Hone your skills and learn your equipment. Know the types of haunting and explain in detail what you think as well as explain your evidence.

Conclusion

Now that you read everything and trust me this is just a little bit of what you need to know, do you still want to be a ghost hunter. No pay, hours upon hours of work, and usually very little respect in the beginning.

This is a passion that I share with my team. I personally want proof of the afterlife before I go there. Now I have a portable hard drive full of data as well as a stack of DVD data disk.

I have been doing this a long time and constantly learning and trying out new equipment and new techniques. It gets expensive but we won't give up. We pay our monthly dues, take any and all donations, and we will be having fundraisers to help raise money for our group.

Now ask yourself, "Will I be just as dedicated to this as they are?"

If your answer is yes, good luck. Most groups disappear within a year, some even less. Now if you're going to be an independent, learn from someone before you go that route. You don't want to embarrass yourself.

The new group I am in likes to work with other groups. I got to work with a person that was in my first group and went off and started his own group. Also I worked with a young lady that first heard me at a local library we would investigate and talk about it. And she started her own group.

It's great to learn from other and I would gladly work with them again.

As I said in the beginning this was going to be brief, we can't share all out secrets, so we come to the end. I thank you for taking this time to read this and I hope you enjoyed it.

Case Files

Remember that since there are so many critics and skeptic you better have case files. You don't want to be caught explaining an event and telling someone what you caught if you don't know where it is. You can burn a CD with everything that you caught or what I did was I got an external hard drive. With that you can store everything in one file.

Now let me tell you about some experiences I have had over the last 12 years.

The first one is one of my wife's favorite. We as a weird family that lives in an area with awesome cemeteries, we went out with a friend and our daughter. When we got to a huge monument my wife wanted to take a picture of this great structure. Funny thing is her camera went off prematurely. We also had a voice recorder with us. Since we were in Illinois we had to scoot out of the cemetery at dusk. Our friend I decided to listen to the audio.

We found that evening more evps than any investigation we have been on. The best, remember the wife taking that picture. Well while she did that our 6 year old was walking around reading the names on the headstones. Now listening to the audio we heard our daughter say "mom" and a voice then my wife said "well at least I got a good picture of it. Now the other voice was a female saying "oh there is a little girl reading in here."

That blew our minds but with all the headstones dating back to the late eighteen hundreds I could understand why this female spirit was impressed.

Now another place that I have been going to for a decade is on a military base. Also this was the commanders' residents. This is the second largest single family building in the army's arsenal.

Not one time going there has disappointed me. From chasing shadows to hearing disembodied voices it has been a great place to investigate. In fact we went there no too long ago and we caught a little girl singing.

What makes this great is we caught it multiple times over the last ten years. We can't say it's a residual due to the fact that there is no actual time period. Plus we have caught a little girl talking to a woman via an evp.

There are so many different locations throughout the years it's hard to pick and choose. From cemeteries to a radio station the use to be a funeral home.

We even have investigated a haunted house attraction that is in a building that use to be a masonic building. We chased shadows, had doors slam, and heard multiple voices. This was truly a great experience.

Now we need to tackle more. And hopefully we continue to work hard to find more evidence and keep working to find a deffinate way to work. Right now we work on theories.

It has taken years to build a reputation and remember one thing can blow it for you. Every investigation and every client has to be handled with professionalism. Sometimes you will be wrong and sometimes you will be over your head. Network and dont be shy to ask for help.

As of late my new group has been working with other local groups. And we have learned different methods and different styles. Remember I was the one who provoked, well Being nice gave me just as many results. I guess you need to choose how you're going to work and change it up sometimes.

So someday I hope that someone will be able to legitimly find a way to bridge the gap between the spirit realm and our world. Then we can see loved ones who have moved on. But until then I will keep collecting evidence and helping those who need it.

Glossary of Terms Used

AFTERLIFE - Life after our physical bodies die. Every culture in the world has their own ideas and beliefs of what the afterlife consist of.

AMORPHOUS - No definite form or shape, often a ghost will appear as a mist or shape.

ANGLES - A being in the supernatural realm that is believed to exist between god and mortal man. They have different purposes and meaning and believed to be guardians over human. Different cultures believe in angles in different ways.

APPARITION - This is when a ghost/spirit takes on a physical form that can be seen or photographed. They are often transparent, faint, and sometimes deformed, and they do not last for a long period of time.

ASTRAL PROJECTION - This is when the spirit of a person travels outside the body to a different location or different plane. Also know out of body experience (obey/oboe)

AURA - The surrounding energy around every living thing. Mood and physical conditions may affect a person's aura.

BANISH - the expulsion of a ghost, spirit, demon, or entities thought to be possessing or haunting a person or location.

BANSHEE - a death omen from Irish culture that those who heard the singing or wailing soon would die.

BATTLEFIELD GHOST - These are often residual ghost that are in areas of great battle. There are not many battle fields that are not hunted.

BENIGN SPIRIT - a spirit that is not harmful or evil to man.

CHANNELING - A proper method of mediums and psychics for communicating to the dead.

CLAIRALIENCE - The psychic ability to receive a message from a spirit by smell.

CLAIRMBIENCE - The psychic ability to receive a message from a spirit by taste.

CLAIRAUDIENT - The psychic ability to receive a message from a spirit by hearing voices or sounds that are normally inaudible to the human ear.

CLAIRSENTIENT - The psychic ability to feel things that are not normally felt by most people.

CLAIRVOYANCE - The ability to see object, event, places, and people not visible through normal sight.

COLLECTIVE APPARITION- The sighting of the same apparition by more than one person.

COLD SPOT- An area that has a large temperature drop from the surrounding area. They are often believed to be made when a ghost or spirit is present.

DEMON - Evil spirit, the minions of the Devil.

DIRECT VOICE PHENOMENON (DVP) - A spirit voice, spoken to people at a séance. Usually the voice comes from a location near the medium.

DISEMBODIED – A spirit function without a body

DISEMBODIED VOICE – A voice that is heard that comes from no physical body.

DIVINATION - The obtaining of future events and the unknown by the use of an outside force.

ECTOPLASM – A solid or vaporous substance, lifelike and moldable.

ELECTROMAGNETIC FIELD (EMF) - A field made by a combination of electric and magnetic energy. Often it is believed that spirits can manipulate these fields, or create their own.

ELECTRONIC VOICE PHENOMENON (EVP) - the use of electronic equipment to record and capture disembodied voices.

EXORCISM - The expulsion of ghost, demons, spirits or other entities the maybe be disturbing.

Ghost - A ghost is believed to be a soul or energy of a person. When someone dies the energy is released from their body and is believed to go to another plain or linger for an unknown period of time.

GREMLINS - A small pesky critter generally friendly but mischievous and involved in many electronically pranks.

HALLUCINATION - A distorted or false perception of an object or event.

HAUNT - A ghost or spirit that returns to a place is said to haunt it.

HAUNTED - A person, place or an object that a spirit is attached.

HAUNTING - Haunting is where a ghost or spirit is attached to a person, place, or object that causes paranormal activity on a regular basis.

LEVITATION - The raising of a person or object into the air without any visible means.

MANIFESTATION - The appearance or form of an entity.

MATERIALIZATION - The formation of a visible ghost or entity on this plain.

ORB - A round shaped ball of energy that produces its own light.

OUIJA BOARD - A messaging board used to contact spirits.

PARANORMAL - Anything that does not represent a natural or normal way of things taking place.

PHANTOM - An apparition or spirit that exists in form only.

PLANCHETTE - The triangle shape instrument that is used with an Ouija board.

VORTEX - An opening into a spirit world. Also maybe triangle shape and is most often imaged as a swirling light.

So You Still Want To Be a Ghost Hunter

www.ingramcontent.com/pod-product-compliance
Lightning Source LLC
Chambersburg PA
CBHW050045080526
44586CB00014B/1464